# A GIFT FOR

MW01609931

## Love Poems by IRVING MELTZ

# CONTENTS

# HOW FORTUNATE

How fortunate I am to be loved by you
And to feel you in everything I do
How fortunate I am to have your grace
And to see the light of your lovely face
How fortunate I am to wake at dawn
And feel your love which draws me on
How fortunate I am that you chose me
To love you for all eternity

CRYING

How plaintive gulls cry out for love
Across the shattered sea
From out the heart of endless love
Their voice cries out to me

The silent beacons swirl and stir
With unborn stars they swoon
Within their fragile hearts they hold
The seeds of sun and moon

# HOW

How can I worry about the tides
When you my friend are by my side?
How can I fret about the night
When your friendly lamp is full of light?
How can I worry about the day
When your promise tears the veil away?
And how can our love not be true
When all I see (my friend) is you?

# EVER

From beginningless beginning
To endless end
I have the company
Of my Friend

From time unwound
To space unbound
Like moon and sun
We are as one

## LEAVES

The very leaves they speak of you
The cloak of night and morning dew
The wind that rushes by my face
The endless aeons of lonely space

# WITH ME

You're with me in the morning
In the rising of the sun
You're with me in the evening
When the long, long day is done
You're with me in the night time
When the stars give out their fires
You're with me when the new day dawns
Our love will never tire

## ALWAYS

Let it be your consolation
That always am I part of you, my dear
Let it be your compensation
To free you from all loneliness and fear

Let it be your understanding
That nobody can prize us apart
Let this be your indication
That always am I (always) in your heart

## MISSING YOU

I miss you more (than I can say)
More than you'll ever know
Every thought of you prolongs
The pain I cannot show

Because the two of us are one
My half has gone to waste
I need the knowledge of your kiss
The sweetness of your taste

One day when we are one again
The world will shine and smile
Until that time (my dearest friend)
My life is in denial

# YOU AND I

You and I were joined at the heart
Till the buffeting universe drove us apart
Till the agony of separation
Drove our love to desolation

## SOMEWHERE, SOMEWHERE

Somewhere, somewhere in the night
My love for you shines long and bright
The pain of longing and sense of belonging
Illuminates the sky like dynamite

Somewhere, somewhere in the day
I know you are not far away
I feel your senses close to me
You are the sand I am the sea

## STRONG

This love is stronger than stronger than strong
Stronger than the washing line
That God hangs stars upon
Stronger than the nails upon which
Galaxies are strung
Stronger than the bolts that keep
The planets from the sun

# SPACE

In this space you've given me
Are moon and mermaid. sand and sea
In this state where we belong
Are verse and vision, sound and song

In this place where rests my mind
Ecstasy hangs in space and time
In this love that's your surround
My soul and yours, in one, compound

## PUT ME

Put me in your pocket
Hide me in your heart
Show me all the little things
You do when we're apart

Place me in your fantasies
Fly me in your breeze
Kill me with your sacred glance
Bring me to my knees

## LOOK ME

Dearest look me in the eye
And say you do no care
The moon has laid her head to rest
And stars for dawn prepare

Darling look me in the eye
And say this is not real
My soul is trammelled in your heart
As stars to rest do steal

## SINCE

Since the dawn of love's conception
Your face has been my recollection
Since the spark that fanned the fire
Your eyes have watered my desire

Since the spark that fanned the flame
My only word has been your name
Since love's single intimation
Your hearts become my consecration

## EASTER

It is Easter afternoon
I have slept half the day.
The sun cascades through my curtains
In a foil wrapped chocolate way

Winter is like a crumpled supermarket voucher
In Easter's clever book
The world is new, and your eyes light the heavens
In a love-filled resurrection look

# EVERYDAY

Everyday I click on you
And the sepia background forms grey out

Everyday I cling to you
And in your face the moon is new

Everyday I take my chances
Beyond the lanes of trite romances

Everyday I take to sleep
And through my hollow dreams you sweep

## TODAY, TODAY

Today, today is a fantasy day
In the sky of my imaginings
The shadows slip away
In the brightness of your face, my dear
Everything is new
In my every spark of happiness
My sights slip into you

## MINE

Mine is the swirling, shifting sea
Mine is the wind that windsweeps me
Mine are the clambering chattering stars
Mine are the eyes of the mountain flowers

Mine are the quiet persistent rhymes
Mine the transcendence of space and time
Mine is the babble of a millions towns
Mine is the love that in you I've found

# FROM NOW

From now until the stars do die
My heart in yours will lullaby
From now until the stars go out
My silent anthem I will shout

From now until the aeons depart
I'll hang your earrings in my heart
From now until the nights switched on
My heart and yours will sing along

## SEEN

I've seen through your soul
To the other side
Now I'm pinned to your heart
Like a butterfly
The places you go
Echo and moan
The dust from your footsteps
Is hallowed in my home

I've seen 'cross your sea
To a further shore
Now my heart is washed up
On the rags that you wore
Oh dear one this world
Was as far as I'd come
Till I saw in your face
The ineffable one

YOU

You play my dreams
I let you win
You turn my key
I let you in
You drown my soul
With your desire
You light my darkness
With your fire

## IT TAKES

It takes a Grace to so unlearn
And make the fires of time unburn
To make the mortal coil unwind
And in its place a fineness find

It takes a Grace to so undo
And make the fires of love shine through
It takes a thread to unthread me
And in your heart forever be

# LANTERNS

Where oh where has wonder gone
And the dazzle of days that made us strong?
Where is the brightness, where the crack
Within the heart of all we lack?

In the instant where we cry
Are echoes of our lullaby
The byways that our hearts explore
Will hang like lanterns from our door

# BITTER BLUE

If you were to love me
I would fly
If you were to kiss me
I would die
If I were to gaze
Upon your face
My soul would disintegrate
In your grace


If you were to draw me
In your life
My rosebud parchment
You'd ignite
If you were to vow
To love me true
Our hearts would merge
In bitter blue

## IF I

If I can understand the stars
Or see some distant galaxy
Their orbs must dwell behind my eyes
And every planet breath in me
Seas must break within my soul
And cities fall within my brain
The labouring heart of endless love
Must beat in my corporeal frame

# JINGLE-JANGLE VALENTINE

There is a place where we two meet
One side stony, one side sweet
There is a place where will meets grace
Where sun and moon meet in one space

There is a place where day and night
Collapse and merge in holy light
There is a falling out of time
A jingle-jangle Valentine

# RESPECTFULLY

Tread the ground respectfully
Your Lord lies in the stones
He took you from your nothingness
And made your blood and bones

He made the earth you walk upon
He made your very feet
He gave you love so you could tell
The bitter from the sweet

## I AM, I AM

I am the trees that stretch their arms
Up to the cold white sky
I am the shining stars that point
And the sound of the seagulls cry

The quiet moon, I am, I am
And the chill of the cold night air
I am the breath within the breath
The stare within the stare

# DRAWN

I'm deeply drawn to you (my love)
To you (my love) I'm deeply drawn
The darkness of my endless nigh
Will find fruition in you dawn

I'm slowly drawn to you (my love)
Slowly drawn into you heart
No bending time or winding rhyme
Can ever keep our souls apart

## BEAUTIFUL

You have made me beautiful
Brighter than the sky
Like a beacon in the night
When the stars fly by

You have made me beautiful
More telling than the air
You've flicked the switch in every face
Illumined everywhere

# WHEREVER

Wherever I go
And whoever I meet
I lie prostrated
At your feet

And whether my eyes
Be opened or closed
Your beauty pierces through my heart
And opens like a rose

# HER

I am her, she is me
I am the roots, she is the tree
I am the dust, she is the ground
I am the roar, she is the sound

Wherever I go, so goes she
Wherein I walk she walks in me
Whatever love I have, she holds
Inside her days my time unfolds

## JUDGEMENT DAY

If all this world should fade and die
Darling there would still be you and I
If all this world should fall asleep
Our autumn vigil we will keep

If all the stars should fade to dawn
In your devotion I'd be born
If all the world should fade away
You'd still be there on Judgement Day

Made in the USA
Lexington, KY
10 February 2014